Galaxies and What We Know about Them! Space Science for Kids

Children's Astrophysics & Space Science Books

PROFESSOR GUSTO
EDUCATIONAL & INFORMATIVE BOOKS FOR CHILDREN
(PRE-K / K-12)

A Galaxy is one big group of stars and other space objects bound together by gravity.

The word 'galaxy' is from the Greek word galaxias, which means "milky", referring to our own galaxy, the Milky Way.

There are around 170 billion galaxies found in the universe. Small galaxies have about 10 million stars while huge galaxies can have 100 trillion stars.

It is believed that there is a massive black hole in the center of each galaxy.

Galaxies are more than 100,000 light years away from each other.

Galaxies are classified into four types depending on its shape.

SPIRAL GALAXY

This galaxy has at least two spiral arms that are circling in a flat disk-shape.

Quick Note:
The arms of
this galaxy
are where
most stars
are formed.

BARRED
SPIRAL
GALAXY

This galaxy is the same as a spiral galaxy but with a long bar in its center.

Quick Note: The best example of a barred spiral galaxy is our galaxy, the Milky Way.

ELLIPTICAL GALAXY

This galaxy is shaped like an elliptical disc.

Quick Note: Elliptical galaxies are large old galaxies and contain less gas as compared to other galaxies.

IRREGULAR
GALAXY

This refers to other galaxies having other shapes aside from spiral, barred spiral and elliptical.

Quick Note:
Some irregular
galaxies are
formed when
other galaxies
crash into
each other.

There is much more to learn about galaxies. Research and have fun!

Printed in Great Britain
by Amazon